KV-245-079

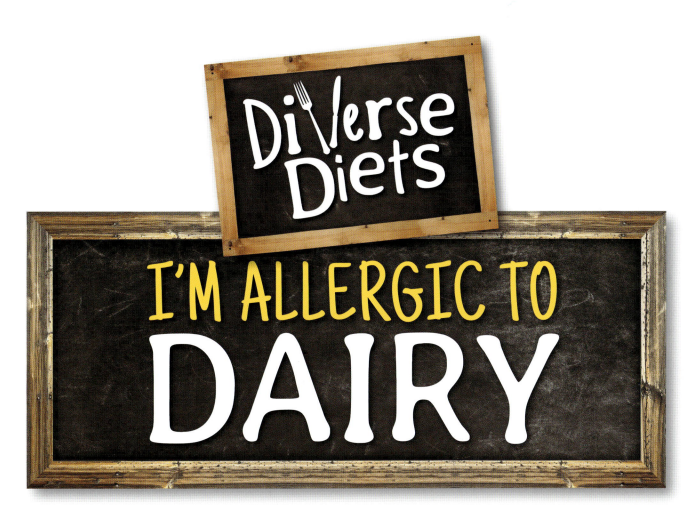

Diverse Diets

I'M ALLERGIC TO DAIRY

By Shalini Vallepur

BookLife PUBLISHING

©2019
BookLife Publishing Ltd.
King's Lynn
Norfolk PE30 4LS

All rights reserved.
Printed in Malaysia.

A catalogue record for this book is available from the British Library.

ISBN: 978-1-78637-726-5

Written by:
Shalini Vallepur

Edited by:
Madeline Tyler

Designed by:
Dan Scase

All facts, statistics, web addresses and URLs in this book were verified as valid and accurate at time of writing. No responsibility for any changes to external websites or references can be accepted by either the author or publisher.

Photo Credits

All images are courtesy of Shutterstock.com, unless otherwise specified. With thanks to Getty Images, Thinkstock Photo and iStockphoto. Front Cover – Vitaly Korovin, SeDmi, Dudarev Mikhail, mything, M. Unal Ozmen, Ines Behrens-Kunkel, Africa Studio, Ku_suriuri, Jane Kelly. 2 & 3 – Dudarev Mikhail, mything, M. Unal Ozmen, Ku_suriuri, Jane Kelly. 4 – Ozgur Coskun. 5 – Albina Glisic. 6 – MarclSchauer. 7 – Jirus Malawong. 8 – margouillat photo. 9 – Designs Stock, Picsfive, Africa Studio, LifetimeStock. 10 – Milleflore Images. 11 – Antonina Vlasova. 12 – M. Unal Ozmen, nuwatphoto, effe45, S_Photo, Anastasiya Samolovova. 13 – Africa Studio, Aleksey Patsyuk, Jiri Hera, Maren Winter, Evgeny Atamanenko. 14 – artjazz. 15 – Studio ART, jujuk suwandono. 16 – LightField Studios. 17 – Binh Thanh Bui, Valery121283, Nils Z, uiliaaa. 18 – Sergiy Kuzmin, visivastudio, sevenke, Phoebe Yu. 19 – Hedez, Flower Studio, Anton Starikov, Iryna Denysova, Anton Starikov, SewCream. 20 – La Bella Studio, Ansty. 21 – Lapina Maria, Makc. 22 – Alexey Smolyanyy. 23 – Pressmaster. Chalk boards – SeDmi. Wood Background – primopiano. Plate – Vitaly Korovin. Notepad – style_TTT.

Contents

Page 4   **Diverse Diets**

Page 6   **What Is Dairy?**

Page 8   **What Is a Dairy Product?**

Page 10   **Smart Swaps**

Page 12   **Strawberry Milkshake**

Page 16   **Keeping up with the Calcium**

Page 18   **Cool Kale Soup**

Page 22   **Living with a Dairy Allergy**

Page 24   **Glossary and Index**

Words that look like **this** can be found in the glossary on page 24.

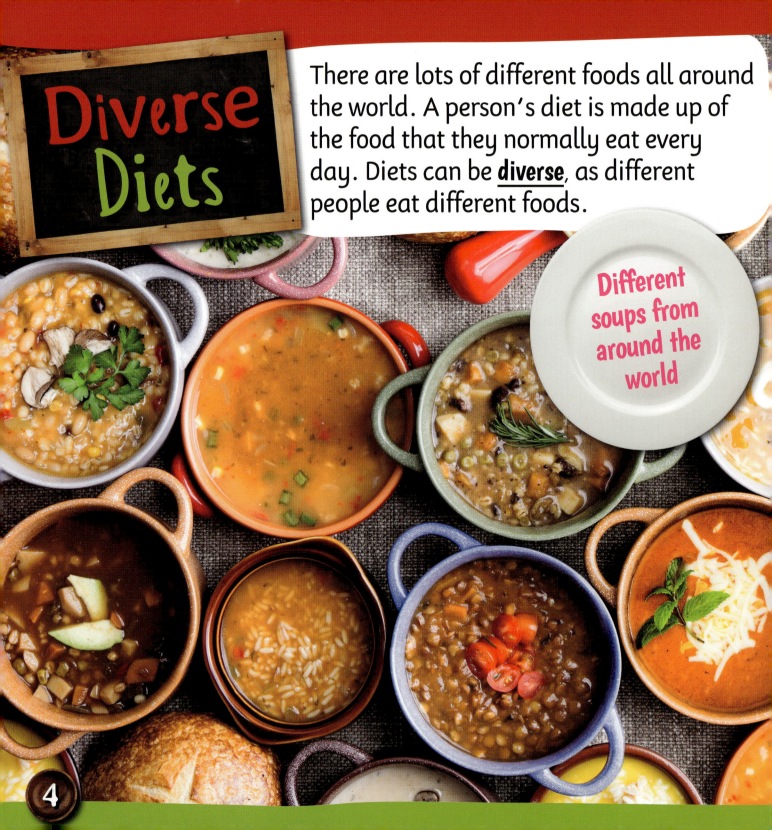

Diverse Diets

There are lots of different foods all around the world. A person's diet is made up of the food that they normally eat every day. Diets can be **diverse**, as different people eat different foods.

Different soups from around the world

Some people may have to change their diet if they have a food **allergy**. If they eat the food that they are allergic to, they could have a bad **allergic reaction**.

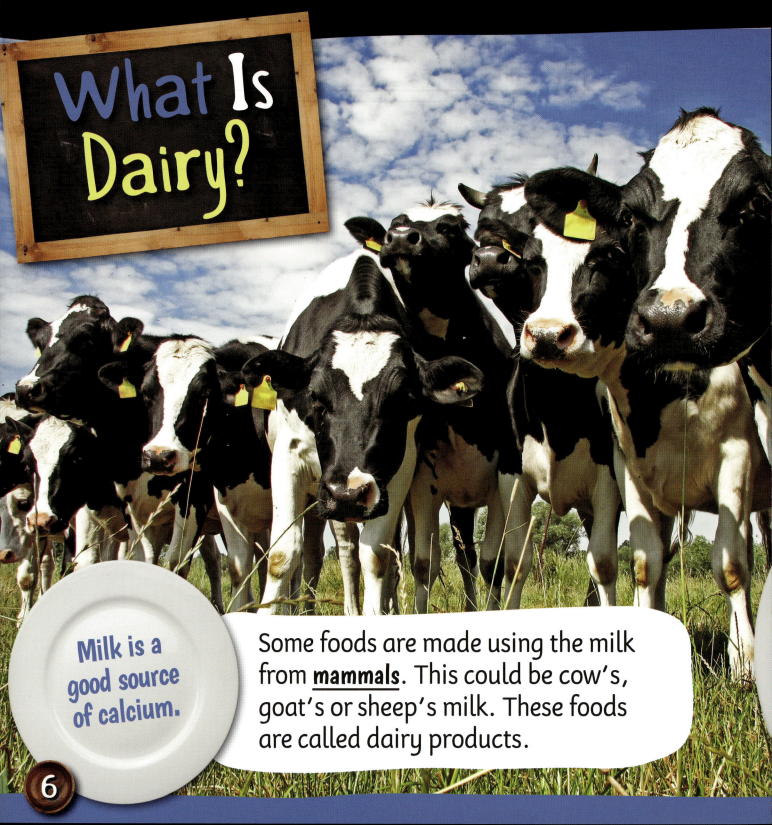

What Is Dairy?

Milk is a good source of calcium.

Some foods are made using the milk from **mammals**. This could be cow's, goat's or sheep's milk. These foods are called dairy products.

If someone has a milk allergy, they could have an allergic reaction when they eat dairy products. They could be sick, cough or have a rash.

If someone is lactose intolerant, their body can't break down the sugar in milk. They could have a tummy ache and be very poorly.

What Is a Dairy Product?

Milk, cheese, cream, yoghurt and butter are all dairy products. People with a dairy allergy must try not to eat these foods.

Do you eat dairy products?

If a food is made from a dairy product, then it is also not safe to eat. This often includes ice cream, chocolate, pizza and cake.

MADE WITH MILK

MADE WITH MILK

MADE WITH BUTTER

CHEESE ON TOP

Can you name any more foods that have dairy in them?

Smart Swaps

There are lots of dairy-free products in the supermarket that are safe for people with dairy allergies. Dairy-free cheeses, yoghurts and creams are made using dairy-free milk.

Dairy-Free Milk

HAZELNUT

WALNUT

SOY

OAT

There are many types of dairy-free milk. You can use dairy-free milk in the same way that you would use dairy milk.

RICE

Let's see what can be made using dairy-free milk…

ALMOND

Strawberry Milkshake

Let's make a healthy and delicious milkshake – with dairy-free milk!

Equipment you will need:

- Measuring jug
- Measuring spoons
- Kitchen scales
- Blender

Ingredients you will need:

- 350 millilitres of a dairy-free milk of your choice
- 350 grams of frozen or fresh strawberries
- 1 tablespoon of maple syrup
- 1 teaspoon of vanilla extract

Measure the ingredients slowly and carefully.

Vanilla

Let's Cook!

Remember to put the lid on the blender before you turn it on!

1. Put half of the strawberries into the blender.

2. Pour the dairy-free milk, maple syrup and vanilla extract into the blender.

3. Blend together.

4. Put the rest of the strawberries into the blender and blend until smooth.

5. Serve!

Try serving the milkshake with extra fruit on top. You can **experiment** with different dairy-free milks and fruit to come up with fun and tasty flavours.

Keeping up with the Calcium

Dairy products are a good source of calcium. Dairy-free milk is sometimes fortified with calcium. This means that is has calcium added to it.

We need calcium to grow and to keep our bones strong.

KALE

ORANGES

People who don't eat dairy need to make sure they have calcium in their diet. These are some dairy-free foods that are good sources of calcium.

BAKED
BEANS

Cool Kale Soup

Let's use kale to get lots of calcium.

HAND BLENDER

KITCHEN SCALES

SAUCEPAN

Equipment you will need:

- Knife
- Measuring jug
- Measuring spoons

Get a grown up to chop, slice and <u>DICE</u> the vegetables.

STOCK CUBES

DAIRY-FREE YOGHURT

Ingredients you will need for four people:

- 25 grams of dairy-free butter
- 1 onion, chopped
- 1 potato, without skin and diced
- 1 litre of vegetable stock
- 400 grams of fresh kale, chopped
- 50 millilitres of dairy-free milk
- 1 tablespoon of dairy-free cream
- Salt and pepper

Let's Cook!

1. Melt the dairy-free butter in the saucepan.
2. Add the onion and potato and cook for ten minutes.
3. Pour in the stock and cook for ten minutes.
4. Add the kale and the dairy-free milk and cook for three minutes.

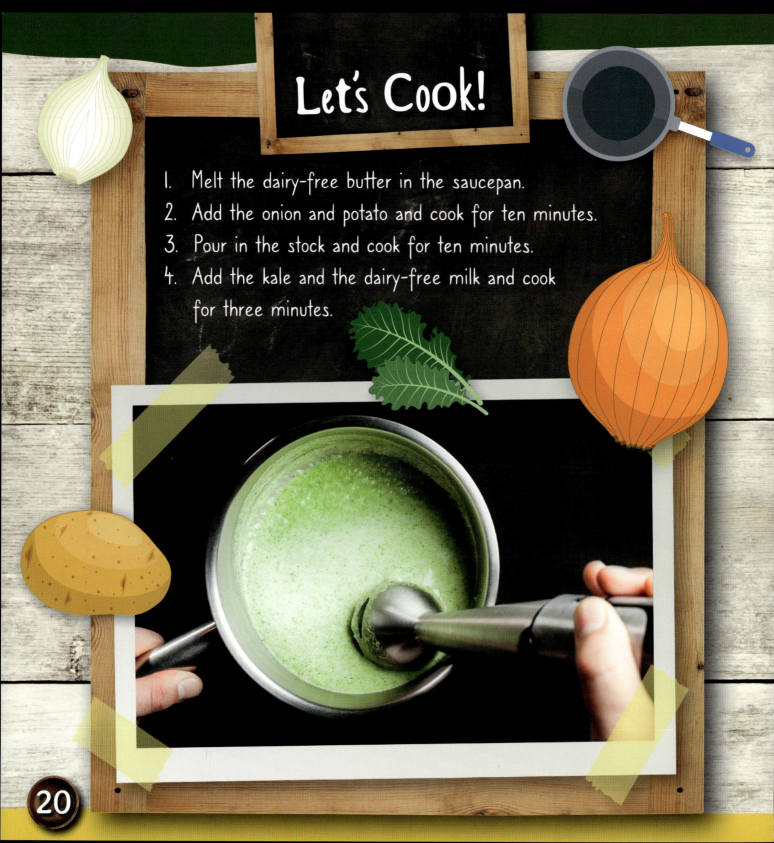

5. Use the hand blender to turn the mix into a soup.
6. Sprinkle in salt and pepper.
7. Pour into bowls and serve with a dollop of dairy-free cream.

Can you make a happy face in your soup with the dairy-free cream?

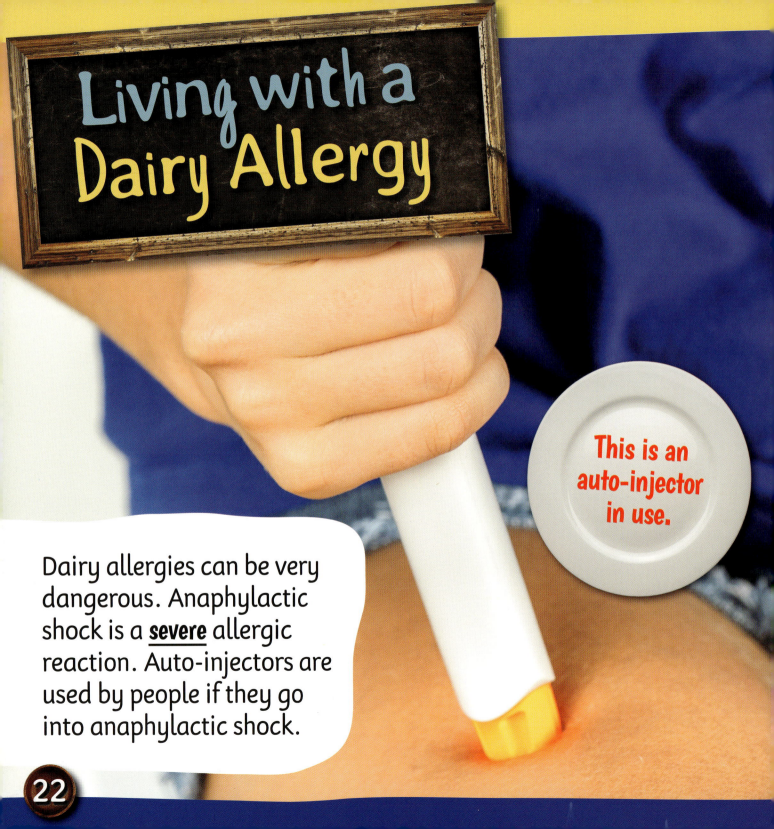

Living with a Dairy Allergy

This is an auto-injector in use.

Dairy allergies can be very dangerous. Anaphylactic shock is a **severe** allergic reaction. Auto-injectors are used by people if they go into anaphylactic shock.

Have you ever looked at a food label? Milk is often labelled as an **allergen** to let people know that it is a dairy product.

Have a look at the label on your favourite food. Does the food contain milk?

Glossary

allergen	things that are harmless for most people, but cause unwanted, bad reactions in others
allergic reaction	getting feelings of illness from something such as nuts
allergy	when the body reacts to something such as nuts, causing feelings of illness
dice	cut into small pieces
diverse	different kinds of things
experiment	to explore and try new things
mammals	animals that have warm blood, backbones and produce milk
severe	serious, very great or intense

Index

allergies 5, 7–8, 10, 22–23
auto-injectors 22
calcium 6, 16–18
cows 6
chocolate 9
cream 8, 10, 19, 21
dairy-free 10–12, 14–17, 19–21

diets 4–5, 17
kale 17–21
milk 6–16, 19–20, 23
milkshakes 12–15
onions 19–20
strawberries 12–14